THE MILLS & BOON®
MODERN GIRL'S GUIDE TO
Working
9 to 5

HQ
An imprint of HarperCollinsPublishers Ltd.
1 London Bridge Street
London SE1 9GF

This hardback edition 2016

1
First published in Great Britain by
HQ, an imprint of HarperCollinsPublishers Ltd. 2016

A catalogue record for this book is
available from the British Library

ISBN: 978-0-00-821233-9

Printed and bound in Italy

Funny, feisty and feminist:
The Mills & Boon Modern Girl's Survival Guides.

Introduction

Dolly is wrong; working 9 to 5 is great. It provides an eight-hour respite from thinking about the meaninglessness of existence. Unless it is one of those jobs that highlights the meaninglessness of existence which, come to think of it, is almost all jobs, so maybe forget I said anything. I'll start again.

For much of history women were confined to the domestic sphere, probably because people in the olden days thought office air conditioning or being near desks would make the fragile female uterus explode. But in 1997, with the release of the Spice Girls' second album, the patriarchy crumbled and women were finally allowed to enjoy all the perks of the workplace that men had enjoyed for years, i.e. stealing stuff from the stationery cupboard and crying in the toilets.

This comprehensive guide will help you to overcome the perils of work. Plus, if you cover the front of the book with pie charts or something, you can read it in your finance meeting and nobody will be any the wiser.

Application

A selection of lies from Clara's CV:

Currently learning Spanish*
(*went to Barcelona for the weekend in 2005;
purchased a wicker donkey wearing a miniature
sombrero; can say 'cerveza, por favor'.)

Passionate about Search Engine Optimisation*
*has not been passionate about anything outside of
cheese or sleeping for almost a decade now.)

Never killed anyone*
(*accidentally killed Pete that time.)

Blue-sky Thinking

Elsie has infiltrated a secret meeting
of the Patriarchy.

They've said 'paradigm shift' and
'robust envelope pushing' a lot.

There were several sterling ideas put forward with
a view to restoring gender equality to 1917 levels.

The one they've decided to go with
is taking control of the weather.

Boredom

Elspeth is trying to concentrate on what
Francine from HR is saying.

There is a stain on the wall behind Francine from
HR. Elspeth thinks about how the stain looks
a bit like a bear.

Elspeth wonders what would happen if the stain
that looks a bit like a bear came to life
and then ate Francine from HR.

Commute

Alternative methods of getting to work that
would still be better than Amy's current commute
on a train franchise we are unable to name
for legal reasons:

Atop an emaciated donkey like you see in those
donkey sanctuary adverts

Through an actual river of treacle

A biplane full of scorpions

Just sitting and waiting for tectonic shifts in the
earth's crust to take her in the right direction

Figure 1:

Figure 2:

Deadlines

Figure 1: What I should be doing

Figure 2: What I am, in fact, doing.

Diversity

A newspaper noticed that there were a lot
of men working at the investment bank.

HR have addressed this diversity issue by
having everyone wear gas masks all the time.

Tina would rather not have to wear the gas mask,
but at least she still has the loos to herself.

Dress Code

'I know this sounds crazy, and I am probably an insane social justice warrior for even mentioning it, but I was thinking that I would quite like to not wear high heels for nine hours a day.'

'Listen, sweetheart, every office has a dress code.'

'Oh well, fair enough. Though I do not one hundred per cent understand why I also have to dress up as a giant egg?'

'Only feminazis refuse to dress up as giant eggs.'

Explaining Your Job To Your Parents

No, Mother, 'The cloud' is not an actual cloud.

Exit Strategy

Janine wants to leave her stressful job, but is worried that she won't find a new one.

She is taking a 'confront your fears' class at the well-being centre.

Kevin is training her to take a leap of faith.

Fridge Etiquette

Things To Mention In A Loud Voice That Might Stop Your Co-Workers Stealing All Your Stuff From The Office Fridge Like They Usually Do:

'Of course, I only drink milk that I've expressed myself.'

'I find making all my sandwiches with roadkill saves time and money – and, honestly, you can't taste the difference.'

'Do you know, I have never once knowingly washed my hands.'

Glass Ceiling

Dear Estelle,

I see where the mix-up has occurred.

When, during your initial interview, you asked if we had 'a glass ceiling' and I said no, what I meant was that we have no upper limit on the size of glass we are prepared to manufacture here at Glass Inc.

The confusion has arisen because you meant glass ceiling in a metaphorical sense, whereas I thought you meant a really big glass, the type of glass you drink out of.

I hope this explains why we will not be promoting you.

INFORMATION

Hot Desking

'So I found yet another mouldy apple core in the drawer, and I can't recall exactly what happened next but, according to Roland from finance, I seem to have abseiled up the walls of the foyer, cut down the experimental Art mobile, soldered it together, then added a hover cushion made from inflated bin bags.

Apparently I started shouting "This is what I think of your f***ing hot desk policy" whilst aggressively gliding across the conference room.

Anyway, to cut to the point, I'm on extended gardening leave. Fancy lunch?'

Invisibility

Mavis has finally realised that she
is invisible at work.

She has conflicting emotions about this.

On the one hand, it has scuppered any chance
of promotions, pay rises or anyone taking any
notice of her in any way.

On the other hand, *she is invisible.* With her new
super power, she can flick vees at the boss, wear
a tiara to meetings and play eight hours
of Minesweeper.

There are advantages to not being seen.

Interviews

What Matilda should have said when asked
what her greatest weakness was:

'Perfectionism. Or maybe caring too much.'

What Matilda actually said when asked
what her greatest weakness was:

'So much to choose from, but on balance: probably
the way I constantly play the sousaphone. It's
actually very disruptive in an office environment.'

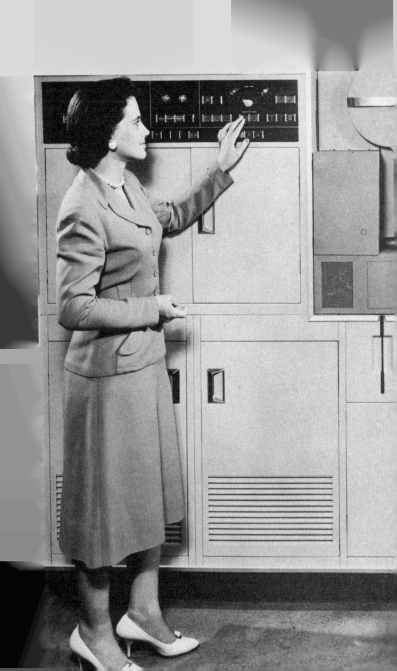

Information Technology

Sometimes Julie sends emails to herself.
She pretends it is her computer sending
romantic messages.

She writes:
'KISS ME, JULIE / TEACH ME THIS EMOTION
YOU CALL LOVE'

and

'I WILL ALWAYS LOVE YOU, JULIE / NOT LIKE THAT
BASTARD DARREN WHO HASN'T RETURNED ANY OF
YOUR CALLS FOR OVER A MONTH'.

Julie's co-workers worry about her.

Jobsworths

It's bad to take your work home with you,
but Andrea *really* enjoys her role as head of
human resources.

Key Performance Indicator

There was a conference. David at the conference said that it was very important for every business to have a Key Performance Indicator.

The good news is that we're doing really well at our Key Performance Indicator.

The bad news is I wasn't really sure what a Key Performance Indicator was so I just wrote down the word 'potato'.

Lateness

This morning?

Bus got hijacked. By a dog. And a monkey. In a little a hat. Might have been a fez, hard to tell. No, I don't think that necessarily makes it a terrorist thing, possibly he just liked little fezzes.

Anyway, long story short, dog trying to steer a hijacked bus with his teeth. Remarkable I'm only forty minutes late, that's the point I'm trying to make.

Lean In

I *think* this is what
Sheryl Sandberg meant.

Male Only Committee

To combat the fact that she's outnumbered
7 to 1 on her company's executive committee,
Betty has decided to make herself appear physically
bigger, like you're meant to do when chased
by a bear.

Or is that bulls?

Either way, it seems to be working.

Meetings

Holly's Review of Today's Strategy Meeting:

Even considered in the context of the disappointing series that has been 'our office meetings' this was a weak instalment. I found the characterisation inconsistent at best and, in the case of Karen from Sales, actively irritating.

orse, the poor reaction to my fantastic joke - where I pretended that I had suffered a brain embolism on account of Chet being so boring - seemed very unrealistic. I think people should have laughed more.

also found the plot of the meeting difficult to follow, ough this may have been because of the nap I took halfway through.

2 stars.

Messing Up Your Big Pitch

Basically, I want you to think Facebook,
but with more mud.

It's going to be very disruptive of
the mud-based economy.

'm looking for £50,000 for a 5% stake. It's a really
exciting opportunity to get in at the ground floor.
We've got an app.

Did I mention how disruptive it's going to be?

Nepotism

Observations About Gareth, Our New Intern:

Gareth has a poor grasp of personal space.

Gareth has a poor grasp of not using other people's clearly labelled mugs.

Gareth has been given a nicer desk than me even though I have been here for seven years.

Gareth doesn't really have a chin.

Gareth has the exact same last name as our VP of Finance.

Office Naps

Virginia has just realised it's the 19th of November, the day that women have to go to work for free for the rest of the year.

This doesn't apply to Jeff at the next desk. He gets paid for all 365 days.

Virginia has taken the executive decision to nap for the next month and a half.

Performance Review

How would you rate your performance in the following key areas this year?

Innovation - I introduced the policy of having an office turkey.

Organisation - I named the turkey 'Robert' and made sure he had a special turkey-sized chair and desk.

ealth & Safety - When Robert pecked that temp in he face I was very proactive. The blood could have caused a nasty slip, but I wiped it all up.

Where could your performance have improved?

More office turkeys.

Pointless Awards

Trophies are a good way of knowing if your job is important. Important jobs like Advertising, Public Relations, Acting and Games Journalism have lots of awards.

Unimportant jobs like Nursing, Firefighting, Cleaning and Teaching have hardly any awards at all.

Michelle, a radiologist, has borrowed this Best Brand Engagement trophy from her more worthwhile friend Dawn. Dawn runs a Twitter account for a company that makes fish paste.

Paperless Office

Head office has decided to go paperless.

After an unseemly scrabble in the stationery cupboard, Shelly has scored a bunch of scrolls, and a pencil that has 'Innovation Imagineer' written on it.

It feels like a hollow victory.

Quitting

Things that Francine has considered as an alternative to another day doing her current job:

Become a meth dealer selling delicious special blue meth (Ethically a bit dubious? I don't own any pipettes)

Something vaguely worthwhile in Africa (I have no discernible skills)

Set up a stock photography archive specialising in pictures of children dressed as turkeys (Adorable! There are no cons, this is a very sound plan)

Security Pass Disaster

Five years.
Five years this pass is valid for.

This will be the picture she will have to wave every morning at Alex, the really hot security guard, for the next five years. Five. Years.

FIVE. YEARS.

Sisterhood

Phyllis has a strategy. Phyllis knows that if she carries a big stapler around she can just pull a sad face and say "sorry, got this important stapling to do" whenever Joan tries to get her to help with that Facilities Management report.

Sisterhood is very important, but you can't be fighting the patriarchy all the time.

Team Building

Mary's recent Ideas for Team Building Exercises
that haven't panned out so well:

1) Getting everyone in the office to read and discuss
Mary's self-published novel.

2) The competitive eating contest with
all the raw eggs.

3) The 'look after a pygmy hippo in
the office for a day' idea.

4) The 'get the team to bury a pygmy hippo before
the man from the zoo turns up to collect the
pygmy hippo' idea.

5) Whatever this 'rolling-metal-cage'
race was supposed to be, Mary can't
even remember.

Unpaid Overtime

It is twenty-nine minutes past five.

But here comes Alan, with the report that's been in his inbox for the last seven weeks.

And he wants to talk about it right this instant.

Even though it could wait until tomorrow.

Or a year from now.

Unsettling Co-Workers

Co-Workers I Find Inexplicably Creepy:

The one who is weirdly cheerful at eight
in the morning.

The one who passive aggressively force-feeds us
the horrible cakes they bring in from home every
single Thursday.

The one who constantly emits this odd tuneless
hum under their breath.

The one who I suspect might just be
a monkey in a coat.

Underwhelming Reality

Job vacancy for an ambitious graduate intern:

Nearly all your travel expenses paid!

And you get to work in the glamorous
world of high-end fashion!

We're hoping to sign Nicole Kidman for
our new campaign!

You won't be working directly with Nicole, no.
You'll more be involved with the 'making-buckets-
for-the-supermodels-to-keep-their-stacks-of-
banknotes-in' side of things.

Competitive benefit package (bucket)!

Vague Sense Of Unease

You definitely logged out of the corporate Twitter account before you sent that tweet. You *definitely* logged out first. Didn't you?

There is absolutely no way that the world's second biggest pharmaceutical company has just posted a tweet about wanting to bang Channing Tatum.

There is no way that the world's second biggest pharmaceutical company posted a tweet about wanting to bang Channing Tatum that included the phrase 'like two puppies fighting to get out of a sack.' as well as an aubergine emoticon.

Oh good God.

Work Day Out

You may never be invited back to the work summer picnic, but at least you'll have the satisfaction of knowing that you arrived in style.

Work-Life Balance

Office life has been getting Jean-Paul down.

He's spent too many nights sleeping under his desk surrounded by empty coffee cups, carpet drool and the soft, despairing tears of a man whose spreadsheets have been publically poo-pooed by vengeful co-workers.

His colleague Simone says he should follow her method for maintaining a work-life balance.

Jean-Paul suspects Simone might be an idiot.

Xmas Party

Bill and Frida had resolved that things wouldn't get weird between them after they snogged in the stationery cupboard at the office Christmas party.

As it turns out, things have got weird.

You're Fired

Hopped up on toner, fired by the lyrics of Cyndi Lauper and happily drunk on the punk rock rhetoric of the Riot Grrrl movement, Patti and Kathleen are blissfully unaware that they've accidentally left five hundred copies of their Girls Just Want To Have Fundamental Human Rights 'zine on the office photocopier for the boss to find exactly half an hour from now.

They will become aware at precisely 9.03 tomorrow morning.

Zero Hours Contract

Patti has found a new job.

It's even better than her last job because now she is on a zero hours contract.

That means Patti gets to be really flexible.

She's flexible about the times she works.
She's flexible about whether she pays the rent.
She's flexible about whether she eats every day.

Flexibility is fun!

About Ada Adverse

Naturally slight of build, Ada's first paid work, age five, was smuggling cigarettes and other contraband through the tunnels beneath the Berlin Wall. Enjoying her taste of early employment she went on to have over a hundred other different jobs, including, but not limited to: delivering eggs to Hollywood's most glamorous celebrities, cartographer, professional wrestler, mystery shopper, designing man-hole covers, and ice-dance choreographer.

She is author of over one hundred books, all of which she dictates from her bath to her man-secretary, Alan.

About Mills & Boon®

Since 1908, Mills & Boon have been a girl's best friend.

We've seen a lot change in the years since: enjoying sex as a woman is now not only officially fine but actively encouraged, dry shampoo has revolutionised our lives and, best of all, we've come full circle on gin.

But being a woman still has its challenges. We're under-paid, exhaustingly objectified, and under-represented at top tables. We work for free from 19th November, and our life-choices are scrutinised and forever found lacking. Plus: PMS; unsolicited d*ck pics; the price of tights.

Sometimes, a girl just needs a break.
And, for a century, that's where we've come in.

So, to celebrate one hundred years of wisdom (or at least a lot of fun), we've produced these handy A-Zs: funny, feisty, feminist guides to help the modern girl get through the day.

We can't promise an end to the bullsh*t.
But we can offer some light relief along the way.